Kelly Clarkson

Behind Her Hazel Eyes

Y Not Girl
Volume 2

A Children's Biography by
Christine Dzidrums

Kelly Clarkson
Behind Her Hazel Eyes

Y Not Girl
Volume 2

A Children's Biography by
Christine Dzidrums

CREATIVE MEDIA, INC.
PO Box 6270
Whittier, California 90609-6270
United States of America

www.creativemedia.net

Cover and Book design by Joseph Dzidrums
Front cover photo by ABC TV

First Edition: April 2013

Library of Congress Control Number: 2013936710

ISBN 978-1-938438-19-6   10 9 8 7 6 5 4 3 2

For Joshua

TABLE OF CONTENTS

"I don't regret one moment of my childhood. I was a shy kid, but that's where my creativity came from."

CHAPTER ONE
"Miss Independent"

The young tomboy hummed the "Indiana Jones Theme" with perfect pitch. She giggled while splashing noisily through treacherous puddles. Texas rain soaked her thick socks and muddied pant legs. Her ponytail bounced as she ran across the wet front lawn.

A few moments later the five-year-old archaeologist scaled a tree effortlessly in pursuit of the Ark of the Covenant. She had to find the treasure before the bad guys discovered it!

Suddenly the young girl heard a hissing coming from below. She looked at the swampy ground beneath her. A sneaky rattlesnake slithered below! He stuck out his forked tongue and glared menacingly at the explorer.

Snakes! She hated snakes!

"Kelly," her mother called. "Time for dinner!"

The tiny child abandoned the fantasy and dashed inside her Fort Worth home. Her dad Stephen Michael and mother Jeanne Ann Rose served food to their waiting children. Kelly's older siblings, fourteen-year-old Jason and twelve-year-old Alyssa, already sat at the table. The entire family looked at the sweat-stained child, who boasted filthy clothes but radiated exuberance over her latest adventure.

"Were you playing Indiana Jones again?" her father finally asked.

On April 24, 1982, Kelly Brianne Clarkson entered the world. Possessing great energy and fortitude, she spent most of her childhood playing outdoors. Kelly wasn't particularly gifted at sports, but she enjoyed playing them. More than anything, though, the youngster loved reenacting scenes from *Raiders of the Lost Ark*. The thrilling adventure flick that centered on a brilliant but non-traditional action hero was her favorite movie ever!

Around five years old, though, Kelly experienced a heavy dose of reality when tension at home grew too enormous to ignore. Her parents had grown apart and argued frequently. Sometimes the small girl sat in her room crying while her folks bickered. Why couldn't her mom and dad just get along?

Just one year later, Kelly's life changed forever when her parents announced they were divorcing. Deep down the youngster believed the decision was for the best, but she still felt devastated to watch her family split into three pieces. Her father and Jason relocated to California, and Alyssa moved in with an aunt. Meanwhile Kelly and her mother settled into a small apartment in nearby Burleson.

Jeanne worked many jobs while pursuing an English degree. Her mother's busy schedule led to Kelly's independence. The youngster washed laundry, prepared meals and cleaned after herself. She developed a strong work ethic and learned to value a dollar.

The chaotic shift in home life greatly affected Kelly. After living in a house with two parents and rowdy siblings, the youngster often found herself alone in a tiny apartment. She sometimes felt sad, confused, lonely and even angry. With her mother's encouragement, Kellbelle, as she was nicknamed, bought a journal to help her cope with all the new feelings. Whenever overwhelming thoughts plagued her, she jotted them down. Writing became a great outlet for her emotions.

Money was tight in the two-person household. To help her mom financially, Kelly once walked throughout her neighborhood searching for homes with unkempt yards and then knocked on the owners' doors.

"Can I mow your lawn in exchange for money?" she always asked politely.

Busy home owners were thrilled to pay a young child for her gardening skills. The youngest Clarkson's weekends soon filled with lawn mowing appointments.

A fervent animal lover, Kelly dreamed of becoming a marine biologist. However one day she watched *Jaws* on television. Steven Spielberg's killer shark thriller scared her so much that she vowed to stay far from the ocean!

Music filled Kelly's life. She often wore headphones attached to a Sony Walkman while doing chores. No Doubt accompanied vacuuming sessions. Alanis Morissette's rock anthems fueled angry dusting. And U2's music worked for any occasion! She also liked Annie Lennox and harbored crushes on Boyz II Men - all of them!

In 8th grade Kelly wanted Reba McEntire concert tickets but the family couldn't afford them. So she consoled herself by listening to the artists' CDs instead. How she dreamed of one day seeing the country legend in concert!

While at Pauline Hughes Middle School, the bored student searched for an extracurricular activity to entertain her and finally settled on basketball. There was just one problem. She wasn't very good at it.

As it turned out, Kelly's true calling found her. One afternoon she sang in the school's hallway when the music director, Cynthia Glenn, approached her.

"You should try out for the choir," the teacher exclaimed.

"I don't have any training," Kelly shrugged.

After some convincing, the teenager joined the choral group and realized how much she loved singing. Choir wasn't the hippest activity, but Kelly never cared what others thought.

The carefree attitude extended toward her wardrobe, too. Strapped for money, she often purchased clothes from thrift shops. One day she even wore a tutu to school.

"Why are you wearing that?" a classmate asked.

"Because I like it," Kelly answered.

"It looks dumb," her peer replied.

"Well you don't have to wear it," she shot back!

PAULINE HUGHES MIDDLE SCHOOL
(Joseph Dzidrums)

When Kelly enrolled at Burleson High School, she found more singing opportunities. Over the years she performed in the musicals *Annie Get Your Gun* and *Seven Brides for Seven Brothers*. The talented girl also portrayed Fiona in *Brigadoon*.

One constant remained throughout Kelly's life. She loved sleeping! The youngster sometimes arrived at school later than her other classmates. She had a horrible habit of sleeping through her alarm!

At age 16, the budding singer applied for a job at Burleson's Hollywood Theater, and a young manager named Jessica Brake hired the friendly applicant. Kelly kept the job for nearly three years, working ticket sales, concessions and the projection booth.

Kelly and Jessica became best friends. The two buddies loved shopping, watching movies and playing beach volleyball. They often hung out with Jessica's sister Halie, too.

The teen also had a trusted friend in a classmate named Ashley. One day Kelly's mom bought a tape recorder for 50 cents at a garage sale and gave it to her daughter. Ashley wrote a sign that said "Recording Studio: Please Do Not Disturb" and taped it her friend's closet. Kelly spent the next hour recording songs inside her makeshift studio.

Jeanne loved making meaningful purchases for her child. Now a first grade teacher, she was a loving parent but not a pushover. Sometimes Kelly wished her mom could be more friend than disciplinarian. Little did she realize at the time that her mother's actions were shaping her into a strong, thoughtful girl who took responsibility for her actions.

Meanwhile others expressed excitement over Kelly's vocal gift when they offered her a massive ovation for her performance at Burleson High's talent show. The enthusiastic reaction triggered the realization that she might win a college voice scholarship, so the talented singer began classical voice lessons.

BURLESON HIGH SCHOOL
(Joseph Dzidrums)

HOLLYWOOD THEATERS- HIGH SCHOOL JOB
(Joseph Dzidrums)

Kelly's hunch proved correct. The University of Texas at Austin, University of North Texas and Berklee College of Music granted her scholarships. Yet when the singer graduated in 2000, she postponed college, believing she could pursue an education at any age.

Instead Kelly juggled several jobs post graduation, hoping to raise money to record a demo that showcased her singing skills. The driven teen flipped pizzas at Papa John's, assembled sandwiches at Subway and worked as a telemarketer.

Not every job turned out well. One day Kelly answered Kirby Vacuum's ad to make $2000 dollars. Needing money for her electric bill, she took the job and then discovered it entailed door-to-door sales. The bummed teen promptly quit.

"I will just live with candles," she thought.

In the meantime, Jessica, now a computer programmer, volunteered to pay for her friend's first demo. The recording earned Kelly contract offers from Jive Records and Interscope Records, but she turned them down, disagreeing with both labels' visions for her.

In 2001 a focused Kelly headed to Los Angeles, where she rented a room and slept on a mattress on the floor. Because the landlord forbade access to the kitchen, the teen purchased a mini-refrigerator for her bedroom.

While in Southern California, the aspiring singer made Frappuccinos® at Starbucks, blended smoothies at Jamba Juice and greeted exercise enthusiasts at 24 Hour Fitness. She even appeared as a television extra in *Sabrina, the Teenage Witch* and *Dharma & Greg*.

Finally Kelly saved enough money to move into an apartment with a roommate. After the excited girls transferred their belongings into the tiny space, their stomachs grumbled from hunger. The famished roommates headed to Chili's restaurant and ordered dinner to go.

When the girls returned, a crowd gathered outside their apartment. Emergency vehicles lined the street. A fire had devastated the complex. Television crews interviewed the performer as she gazed at the burned structure in a daze. Kelly lived in her car for three days before she finally drove 24 hours straight home to Texas.

Back in Burleson the broke youngster earned 13 dollars an hour peddling Red Bull energy drinks. Eventually, though, she became a cocktail waitress at Hyena's Comedy Nightclub. The difficult job exposed her to many rude, drunk customers but the tips provided decent earnings.

Thankfully, that waitressing gig would be the final working class job of Kelly's life.

"I want to be an American Idol because I like to perform."

CHAPTER 2
"You Found Me"

One afternoon Jessica's mom Terry heard a radio spot advertising auditions for *FOX*'s new singing competition, *American Idol*. The show sought to find the nation's best undiscovered voice and would host Dallas auditions.

Later that night when Kelly visited the Brake home, she munched on pizza rolls while her friends described the tryouts. Stung by her Los Angeles experience, the singer shrugged off the opportunity, so Jessica filled out an audition form and handed the paper to her friend.

"What are you doing sitting around?" she asked. "Do it."

"I'm never going to make it," Kelly protested. "I'm not as pretty as the other girls. I'm not as skinny as the other girls."

"Just be yourself," her friend advised. "If you show you're silly and sweet, they'll love you."

Kelly finally relented. Okay. Fine. She would audition. What could it hurt?

The night before tryouts, nerves consumed her. What if the alarm didn't wake her? The nervous singer hopped out of bed and headed to Jessica's house.

Moments later the twenty-year-old tiptoed across the Brake's lawn and tossed a pebble at Jessica's second-story bedroom window. A minute later, her sleepy-eyed friend appeared.

"I don't want to oversleep!" Kelly whispered. "You have to keep me awake."

Jessica nodded understandingly. The girls spent the next few hours chatting about fluff as the big audition neared.

"I was broke and didn't want to go back to living in my car," the performer told the *Daily Mail*. "My main aim was to pay the electricity bill."

When Kelly arrived at the tryout, she wore her own design, a blouse made from an old pair of pants. After sailing through round one, she would next face three celebrity judges: '80s pop star Paula Abdul, music producer Randy Jackson and A&R executive Simon Cowell.

Kelly waited anxiously in a holding area. Television cameras captured the drama as singers entered the audition room and exited in tears. They all claimed that the British judge (Cowell) was brutally honest and impossible to please.

"I don't want him to be mean to me," Kelly thought. "That's my only goal."

While waiting by the audition room, the *Idol* hopeful chatted with the show's hosts, Brian Dunkleman and Ryan Seacrest. The kind duo distracted the singer until producers finally summoned her to face the judges.

The three personalities watched Kelly carefully when she entered the room. Was she the next *American Idol*?

"Hi Kelly," Paula smiled.

"Hi," Kelly answered. "I'm a big fan, by the way."

"Thank you very much," the famous singer replied.

AMERICAN IDOL CONTESTANT
(Lee Roth RothStock PR Photos)

AMERICAN IDOL SEASON ONE TOP 7 FINALISTS
(Lee Roth RothStock PR Photos)

Kelly then sang two diverse selections, Etta James' "At Last" and Madonna's "Express Yourself."

"I worked on that song with Madonna," Randy remarked.

Simon and Paula groaned and feigned sleep over the producer's boastful comment. He loved dropping names.

"I love me," Randy smiled.

"You should be a star," Kelly urged. "You should try out!"

Before the young lady knew it, she and Randy traded places. Kelly sat beside Paula and Simon while the judge "auditioned" with R. Kelly's "I Believe I Can Fly."

"What do you think?" Kelly asked Simon. "Hollywood?"

"Not in a trillion, billion years," the cranky judge replied.

Once the charade ended, Kelly held her breath and waited for the judges' decision. In the end, they voted unanimously to send her to the next round.

"I was so happy because the British man didn't make me cry," she later told *American Idol Rewind*.

A few weeks later, Kelly returned to Hollywood and survived round three. For the fourth phase, she would sing on live television.

American Idol went live. The excited Texan and 29 other performers would compete for ten finalist spots, which would be decided by the viewing audience's votes. Of those ten contestants, one would win *American Idol*.

Wearing a black pantsuit, the talented vocalist belted out Aretha Franklin's "Respect." She impressed with her strong vocals and advanced to the top ten! The Dixie Chicks' Natalie Maines also became a big fan, throwing her support behind the phenomenal singer.

Home viewers would now eliminate one performer weekly until just one contestant remained. That person would earn a million-dollar recording contract! The Burleson native now had a 10% chance of winning *American Idol*. She seized the opportunity by performing flawlessly for the remainder of the show's run.

During top ten week, Kelly struggled with laryngitis but delivered a remarkable "You're All I Need to Get By."

"Kelly, I think you just raised the game, haven't you?" Simon asked. "As they say in Texas, y'all did a great job!"

The crabby judge's praise flabbergasted Kelly. Meanwhile, *FOX* was also surprised to discover they had a major hit on their hands. *American Idol* positively soared in the ratings.

For the next few weeks, Kelly wowed music lovers with spectacular renditions of "Natural Woman" and "Don't Play That Song (You Lied)." Her most memorable performance came during Big Band Week when she tackled "Stuff Like That There," complete with a '40s hairstyle.

"You're one of the most natural great singers I've heard in a long time," Randy praised.

"You are a triple threat," Paula complimented. "I could see you on film. I could see you on stage. You have it all, Kelly."

"Thank God you entered this competition," Simon exclaimed. "I truly believe you are going to become a huge star at the end of this show."

Kelly experienced one major disappointment during her *American Idol* stint, though. The maid of honor missed Jessica's wedding due to a television commitment. On that afternoon she listened to the bride's wedding over the phone.

As *Idol*'s finale quickly approached, grandparents, children, moms, dads... Everyone debated who would snatch the title. Even news outlets got into the act.

"The sweet, friendly Texan is blessed with a set of cosmic pipes that will win it all," the *Detroit Free Press* predicted.

Although Kelly loved performing for millions every week, the television gig took its toll. The contestants rehearsed, filmed commercials, granted countless interviews and attended promotional appearances. By the time performance night arrived, they felt utterly exhausted.

AMERICAN IDOL FINALS
(Lee Roth RothStock PR Photos)

Nevertheless, Kelly continued earning raves from the judges. During the top four round, she impressed with "It's Raining Men" and "I Surrender."

"I think you've just put yourself up in the same league as Celine and Mariah Carey," Simon announced.

After Tamyra Gray's surprising elimination the following night, three finalists remained. Kelly, Justin and karaoke business owner Nikki McKibbin would challenge for the title. Before the competition continued, producers released the trio for a hometown celebration.

When Kelly returned to Burleson she swirled about town giving interviews and visiting with friends and family. Later hundreds of screaming fans greeted her at her alma mater.

"To everyone else Kelly may be a celebrity but to us she's always going to be Kelly," her mom claimed.

Wherever the contestant went, people asked about Simon. Was he just as cranky off-camera? Did she like him?

"I don't think Simon is too harsh," Kelly told the *Daily Mail*. "There are critics all over the music industry and you have to be able to handle that."

As expected, viewers eliminated Nikki several days later. Kelly would face Justin for bragging rights as the first *American Idol*. Would the hunk or the sweetheart win?

Before the big finale, Kelly, Justin and the judges attended the *2002 MTV Video Music Awards* and presented Avril Lavigne with a Best New Artist trophy. Reporters surrounded the television stars backstage. One man begged Kelly to sing

"Happy Birthday" to him but an *Idol* representative made her decline, citing that she needed to protect her voice.

On the last competition night, *American Idol* moved to the Kodak Theatre, home of the Academy Awards. The finalists sang two original compositions, "A Moment Like This" and "Before Your Love." Whichever singer won the competition would release the first song as their debut single. Burleson's hometown girl sang each ballad beautifully, earning huge applause. All three judges claimed she gave the best performances.

Kelly also accumulated supporters outside *Idol*'s studio. *Will and Grace*'s Megan Mullally revealed that she voted repeatedly for Kelly on one phone line, while her husband voted on another.

On *American Idol*'s finale Kelly wore blue jeans, a soft pink blouse and a maroon blazer. A thousand well wishers gathered at Burleson High to cheer her on.

"America needs to be proud that Kelly was chosen," choir teacher Debbie Pesnell told the *Dallas Morning News*. "She's proud to be from Burleson. She deserves this."

"She's so unassuming," she added. "She's just a star in her own right."

Nearly 18 million people watched the two-hour event. Kelly and Justin sang solos and teamed for a duet, "It Takes Two." A best of/worst of segment aired. Other finalists performed, too.

Finally Kelly and Justin stood center stage for the big announcement. They gripped one another's hand as Ryan opened the envelope to announce the victor.

AMERICAN IDOL CHAMPION
(Lee Roth RothStock PR Photos)

"The winner of *American Idol* 2002 is…Kelly Clarkson!"

The twenty-year-old wept with relief and happiness as the Kodak audience roared. Burleson's celebration reached deafening levels. The hosts asked the champion how she felt.

"I'm pretty much thinking how I'm going to sing this next song while I'm crying," Kelly answered. "I don't know what to say!"

"I am so happy with tonight's decision," Justin gushed. "No one deserves it more than this woman right here, Kelly Clarkson."

"Congratulations, America." Ryan Seacrest announced. "You made this happen. This is your idol."

Kelly took the microphone and sang her coronation song, "A Moment Like This." Peering out in the audience, she spotted her mother crying uncontrollably and summoned all her concentration to remain focused.

As she neared the end of her song, fireworks exploded above the stage. Contestants congratulated the champion while confetti rained everywhere. Americans celebrated at home.

A star was born.

"I have plenty to be thankful for this year...no pun intended."

CHAPTER 3
"Ready"

"I want to make songs I'm proud of," Kelly told *Entertainment Tonight*.

After her victory, Kelly embarked on a whirlwind publicity tour. She graced talk shows, granted interviews and sang at several important events.

Meanwhile *American Idol* enjoyed overwhelming popularity. *FOX* ordered a second season, merchandising sales went into overdrive, and RCA released the *American Idol Greatest Moments* CD.

Kelly and the other finalists set forth on a 28-city tour called *American Idols Live*. As the main draw, Kelly received the lineup's final slot. She felt thrilled to get paid for touring the country as a singer. During the 150 minute show, the new star sang "Natural Woman," "Respect," "A Moment Like This" and "Before Your Love." She also performed in the all-girl number "Free Your Mind."

"Clarkson and home-grown Tamyra Gray, the Takoma Park native, have voices of fetching texture and charisma to spare," raved *The Washington Post*.

Now earning good money, the generous performer used part of her $200,000 advance to buy Jessica her dream car, a Corvette. She also purchased a home for her mom.

"I didn't grow up with a lot of money," Kelly told *GMTV*. "So it was cool to give back to everyone who helped me get to where I am now."

RCA initially announced that the *American Idol* winner would release their album in November. Handlers wanted to strike while the iron was hot. Except Kelly insisted that she record a quality album, so the label pushed back the release date.

"I put my foot down," she told the *Rocky Mountain News*. "I said, 'Do you want it now or do you want quality?'"

The label did release her first single on September 17, though. "A Moment Like This" debuted at number 52 on *Billboard's Hot 100* and shot to number one a week later. The surge broke the Beatles' record for the biggest leap to number one. In the end, the song sold over one million copies.

Meanwhile Kelly and producers carefully crafted her debut CD, *Thankful*. The name originated from the work's ninth track and seemed a fitting title.

"There was no other word to describe my year," Kelly told *USA Today*. "I'm thankful in every way, shape and form."

On April 15, 2003, RCA Records released Kelly's first album. The nervous singer wondered if people would like *Thankful* and got her answer a few days later.

"Congratulations!" her manager announced. "You're at the top of the charts."

Thankful sold 297,000 copies during its first week, more than Madonna's *American Life* did a week earlier. After debuting at number one, it eventually reached double-platinum status, selling over three million copies worldwide.

Kelly used her album's liner notes to thank her family, friends, fans and music professionals. The classy performer also acknowledged *Idol's* nine other finalists. Meanwhile critics thanked her for delivering a strong work.

"Clarkson has a stunning voice - scuffed Texas-soul mixing Dusty Springfield's emotiveness with Aguilera's delicate power. When the material is melodic, as on the country-western/R&B ballad "The Trouble With Love Is," Clarkson's voice soars." - *The Philadelphia Inquirer*

"Miss Independent" became the album's first single, a catchy tune originally intended for Christina Aguilera and then Destiny's Child. Kelly premiered the gritty song on *American Idol* and earned a standing ovation from all three judges!

The fiery anthem follows a strong, wary girl who finally finds love! The story resonated with the singer who reworked some lyrics to suit her better.

"It's funny when the song came into play, I was going through that kind of thing," Kelly told *MTV*. "I've always been guarded about work and career, so it was easy to write the bridge to the song."

"Miss Independent" achieved great success, reaching number nine on *Billboard's Top 100* chart. It even triumphed in other countries, like England, Australia and Germany.

Thanks to her increased popularity, Kelly now found that people recognized her all the time. Fans asked for autographs whenever she went out!

The new celebrity received so much fan mail that an entire team handled it. She also changed phone numbers and email addresses after both were revealed online. Sometimes guys even proposed to her!

THE 2003 TEEN CHOICE AWARDS
(Lee Roth RothStock PR Photos)

"Dude, you don't even know me!" Kelly thought.

The Texan spent the next several months traveling while promoting *Thankful*. Of the many fascinating destinations she visited, Kelly liked Spain best, especially its gothic architecture. Mostly she felt thrilled to discover that her fan base extended outside her country's borders.

"Whether I'm in Germany, Ireland, France or America, the fans know the songs," she told *The Mirror*.

On her first European trip, Kelly met many celebrities and even interviewed actress Reese Witherspoon! The girls immediately clicked thanks to their Southern backgrounds.

"I'm a huge fan of yours," Reese gushed.

Kelly also attended an Annie Lennox concert and met her favorite singer backstage after the show. The young performer even learned helpful warm-up exercises from her hero.

"Low" marked *Thankful*'s next single. The singer had a blast filming the music video in a California desert. Although the song performed fair business in America, it reached number two in Canada and remained Kelly's favorite song from her debut album.

RCA released "The Trouble with Love Is" as the album's final single. The song describes love's pros and cons and received additional exposure when the movie *Love Actually* featured the tune.

Incidentally *Thankful* contained a popular fan favorite, "You Thought Wrong," a fierce duet with Tamyra Gray. Kelly actually fought for the song's release but her label declined to release the tune. Nevertheless the singers delighted fans when they performed the tune on select dates of Kelly's first tour.

In summer of 2003, 20th Century Fox released *From Justin to Kelly*, a light summer fare featuring the top two *Idol* finalists. Contractually obligated to appear in the movie, Kelly played a singing waitress who falls for Justin's college hunk during spring break in Fort Lauderdale, Florida. The *Idol* pals sang several tunes, including an original duet called "Timeless."

"I think it's a really fun movie," the new actress told the *Chicago Sun Times*. "I had a blast making it. I can't wait until the fans get a chance to check it out."

In true Kelly fashion, though, she originally resisted playing the cute, romantic lead. Those parts didn't excite her.

"I'd rather do character acting," she told *USA Today*. "I'd rather be the sidekick, the weird girlfriend or someone psychotic. My dream role is like Kathy Bates in *Misery*."

Later that year Kelly screamed excitedly during a radio interview upon hearing she earned a Grammy Award nod. The rookie nominee competed for Best Female Pop Vocal Performance against Christina Aguilera, Dido, Sarah McLachlan and Avril Lavigne. Although Christina ultimately snatched the top prize, the *Idol* champ felt thrilled to be in the company of four amazing women.

Around the same time, Kelly bought her first home, a 12-acre Texas ranch. She loved having the privacy it afforded her, even if she didn't exactly consider herself a farmer.

"I love the countryside but I'm not John Wayne or anything," she joked to talk show host Ellen DeGeneres.

The fun-natured girl even built a go-kart track on the property and hosted several cool racing days. She also utilized the land to house rescue horses, goats and donkeys.

In addition, Kelly purchased a Los Angeles beach house, since she often worked in the city. Among trivial indulgences, the artist also bought a big-screen TV and an Acura SUV.

Running Kelly's career proved a full-time job for many people. The young woman's team consisted of trusted friends and family, including her brother as a personal assistant.

"We've only come to know each other again in the past five years, but we're so spookily similar in our mannerisms," she told *The Sunday Mail*. "I still look up to him."

In early 2004 Kelly began a joint tour with *American Idol* season two runner-up Clay Aiken. *The Independent Tour* played 30 cities across the United States, like Tampa, Los Angeles, Long Island, Las Vegas and Chicago. The beloved Texan also performed solo stops in Houston and Austin. The stars alternated headlining arena dates and even joined forces on a duet to Journey's "Open Arms."

Kelly liked Clay. He was unpretentious and laid-back, like her. They became fast friends and passed travel time by playing Scrabble on the tour bus.

"Barefoot and playing acoustic guitar, Clarkson displayed a soulful, versatile voice," raved *The Boston Globe*.

Despite headlining a major tour, Kelly resisted celebrity treatment. When hotel bellboys picked up her luggage, she'd stop them and carry it herself!

"I got into this for the right reasons," she told *USA Today*. "I don't care about fame. I honestly don't give a flip. I hate limos, and I like going places by myself. My friends keep me levelheaded. Being a star has never been a huge deal to me."

On the other hand, Kelly still gushed over other stars. She wanted to be best friends with Meryl Streep and harbored several celebrity crushes, like Matthew Perry, David Boreanaz, Kyle Chandler, Ewan McGregor and Hugh Jackman.

Kelly even joined film history when Steve Carell uttered her name in *The 40-Year-Old Virgin*. In an improvised scene, the title character waxes his chest. When the process becomes painful, he screams nonsensical phrases, like "Kelly Clarkson!" The singer didn't know about the reference until she went to the movies with friends. As she settled into her seat, a preview for the comedy began. The confused Texan looked at her buddies.

A THANKFUL KELLY
(Lee Roth RothStock PR Photos)

"Did y'all hear my name?" she asked.

"I guess you've made it when Steve Carell yells your name," she later laughed.

On one neat occasion Kelly bought Aerosmith concert tickets. A Steven Tyler fan, she squealed when the frontman mentioned her during the concert and invited her backstage. She laughed in disbelief when Steven said he voted for her.

In more celebrity encounter news, Kelly even sang with Reba McEntire during the television special *American Idol: Las Vegas*. The singer wept before taking the stage with her hero, remembering how years earlier she'd dreamed of seeing the superstar in concert but couldn't afford tickets.

And now? Now somewhere, little girls dreamed of seeing Kelly Clarkson in concert!

"If fame is your sole purpose in life, that's a pretty big void you're trying to fill."

CHAPTER 4
"Respect"

For album number two, Kelly focused on one of her big strengths: versatility. She sampled many different genres.

"I'm going different styles on this album -- rock, soul, big band, Motown," she told *The Spokesman-Review.*

On November 30, 2004, RCA released Kelly's sophomore effort, *Breakaway*. The album lived in the *Billboard 200* for an astonishing 61 weeks and sold over six million copies. Critics loved it, too.

"Clarkson shows her fans a more mature attitude and voice." - *Dayton Daily News*

"Unlike her angst-filled peers, Kelly Clarkson really can sing. She has a voice full of soul, range, emotion and personality." – *Jerusalem Post*

Breakaway's first single, the title track, featured a country flavor. With a co-writing credit by Avril Lavigne, the song also appeared in *The Princess Diaries 2*. The breezy tune became a huge number one hit and a constant staple on Top 40 radio.

"This song was different from everything I've done," Kelly told *The New York Beacon.* "People didn't know it was me!"

"'Breakaway' is a simple song, and its simplicity is what's beautiful about it," she added.

The artist began the *Breakaway Tour* in Tulsa, Oklahoma. Thrilled to headline her first solo tour she oozed enthusiasm about playing live shows.

"Nothing makes me happier than being on the road," she remarked. "I can't wait to see fans and perform my material."

The grueling tour lasted many months but she cherished witnessing people singing along to her songs. Sometimes their passion surprised her, like when one fan kept screaming for her.

"Wow," Kelly finally joked. "You're not going to have a voice tomorrow. It sounds like someone is killing you!"

Breakaway's second single, the angry anthem "Since U Been Gone," details a girl's feeling of freedom after her relationship ends. The fun sing-along became the year's biggest hit but it almost didn't get recorded.

"I was like, 'It's a catchy song, I could sing the heck out of it, but I don't think this is my vibe,'" she remarked.

Rather than rejecting the song, Kelly infused the tune with a greater rock edge. She used Aerosmith and Janis Joplin as inspiration for the song's feisty attitude.

After a steady climb up the *Billboard Hot 100*, "Since U Been Gone" finally nabbed the top spot and stayed there for a staggering six weeks. A worldwide success, the song established its singer as a powerhouse in several foreign markets, too.

The popular single even led the performer to two *MTV Video Music Awards*, Best Female Video and Best Pop Video. Kelly's *American Idol* family expressed delight with her success.

"We're proud, we're happy, and it's nice that she remembers the show," Simon Cowell told *The Associated Press.*

Kelly's next single, "Behind These Hazel Eyes," was her favorite *Breakaway* song. The edgy tune about a content girl who realizes her ex-boyfriend regrets their breakup became the album's fourth smash. Many correctly guessed that the singer modeled the number after her ex-boyfriend Graham Colton.

"I wrote 'Behind The Hazel Eyes' about my last boyfriend," she admitted. "I'm not worried about people knowing whom these songs are about. I'm a normal 22-year-old girl, and if someone breaks my heart, I'm gonna write about it. I'm putting out my diary basically. It's a very personal thing."

Speaking of highly personal, "Because of You" became *Breakaway's* fourth single. Kelly wrote the aching song at age 16, when she experienced difficulty coping with her parent's tumultuous relationship. The lyrics describe a young girl wracked with insecurity but determined to stop her family's cycle of bad habits. The songwriter fought for the song to be included on her second album before finally winning the battle. Then she cleared the tune's delicate subject matter with her family.

"That's probably the most personal song I've ever written," she told the *Post-Tribune*. "It's about growing up in a broken home, which a lot of people do."

Kelly hoped to reach young fans going through similar, painful family situations. She wanted them to know they were not alone.

"I have a younger audience," she remarked on *RoveLive*. "Little girls and little guys don't know how to handle it when their parents get divorced. They don't know what to do, or feel kind of odd. It's something to help you feel more accepted."

KELLY BREAKS AWAY
(Lee Roth RothStock PR Photos)

Residual nerves and vulnerability stemming from the studio's dislike of "Because of You" engulfed Kelly. The fretful singer battled a nervous stomach the entire day. It meant so much that others appreciated her effort. She compared the single's release to the experience of telling a guy she liked him and waiting that few crucial seconds to hear his response!

Thankfully music lovers propelled "Because of You" to #7 on the *Billboard Top 100* chart. As a final triumph, Kelly performed the smash before a star-studded audience at the *48th Grammy Awards*. She even recorded it as a duet with Reba McEntire, where it reached #2 on the *Hot Country* chart.

It seemed wherever Kelly went, people thanked her for writing "Because of You." Thanks to the song, many felt comforted to learn that their family struggles were not uncommon. It inspired them to know that their hero also went through family friction and emerged even stronger.

"I want to be on the Grammys," a young Kelly once exclaimed. "That would be so cool. To perform for people that you looked up to since you were little, that's the highest."

On February 8, 2006, Kelly arrived at the Los Angeles Staples Center for the *48th Annual Grammy Awards*. Accompanied by her childhood friend Ashley Donovan, the nominee wore a black strapless gown. She begrudgingly walked the red carpet, even if the celebrity tradition unnerved her.

"I'd rather watch a movie or ten episodes of *Lost* than go out," Kelly told *The Sunday Mail*. "I feel awkward on a red carpet - I can't pose like a model, it's just not me."

About an hour later, Alicia Keys and Stevie Wonder walked onto the stage to present Best Female Pop Vocal

Performance. The humble Texan was in the same category as Mariah Carey, Sheryl Crow, Bonnie Raitt and Gwen Stefani.

"And the Grammy goes to Kelly Clarkson!"

Her first Grammy! Kelly took a beat to let the realization hit her. After hugging Ashley, she walked to the podium and delivered a speech she'd dreamed about since childhood.

"Oh God, I'm terrible at speaking when I cry…so sorry. Thank you so much. Thank you everybody that has supported me this year, including my record label and my management. I love you, Jeff Kwatinetz. Thank you to my date Ashley Donovan, my first producer in my closet back home when I was kid. Thank you to my mom. Thank you, Mom. I'm sorry I'm crying again on national television. Thank you to the fans. Thank you to everyone who worked on my record. And just thank you so much. You have no idea what this means to me, so thank you so much."

Later Teri Hatcher and Michael Bublé announced Best Pop Vocal Album. The contenders included Fiona Apple, Kelly Clarkson, Sheryl Crow, Paul McCartney and Gwen Stefani.

"And the Grammy for Best Pop Vocal Album goes to *Breakaway* - Kelly Clarkson."

Another Grammy! Kelly shook her head in disbelief. She used her second victory to acknowledge her idols in attendance that night, like Bonnie Raitt and Gwen Stefani. After walking backstage, she ran straight into Madonna! The dazed singer reached to shake the Material Girl's hand, but the pop icon hugged her instead!

"I just met Madonna!' she giggled afterward.

Meanwhile Kelly's *American Idol* friends felt thrilled with her success. She had easily emerged as the show's biggest success story.

"I'm really happy for her," Randy Jackson told *The Cincinnati Post*. "She's really over the moon because I think she thought she'd never win it."

Perhaps television's first *American Idol* never thought she'd win a Grammy. But she dreamed it might happen.

GRAMMY WINNER
(Glenn Harris PR Photos)

"My December is the story of me over the last couple of years, going through great times, bad times, and bitter times."

On February 27, 2007, Kelly announced her third album, *My December*. The ambiguous title stirred interest.

"You know when it's the new year, you just feel like you need a fresh start?" the singer asked *CosmoGirl*. "Well, it was that feeling for me. When I started writing [this album], I needed a fresh start and it felt like the right title."

The new work marked a new direction for the popular singer. *My December* contained darker, edgier songs than previous efforts. Songs were less pop, more blues.

"It's like a throwback to Janis Joplin, Sly, some of (the new songs) are a little Prince-ish," Kelly revealed to *The Associated Press*. "It's still got the whole rock-pop vibe, but certain songs have an extreme amount of soul as well."

Kelly co-wrote *My December*'s 13 tracks during her *Breakaway* tour, scrawling lyrics constantly. Whether at home, on a plane or at a restaurant, she jotted down thoughts. Sometimes the process consumed her.

"The moment a song comes to me, I have to get it out," she told *Contactmusic.com*. "I have a hard time sleeping, because a lot of those times are at night."

After listening to *My December*, Clive Davis felt the songs were too dark and negative. Rumors circulated that he wanted the album scrapped and new music recorded. Kelly fought hard for the album's release.

"Like any family we will disagree and argue but, in the end, it's respect and admiration that will keep us together," she remarked.

When the album hit stores on June 22, 2007, loyal fans snatched up copies, and reviewers embraced it.

"With *My December*, Kelly Clarkson has proven she has the courage and the diversity to helm what is undoubtedly going to be a golden career." - *CinemaBlend.com*

"Kelly Clarkson's third major label release *My December* is her best offering so far." – *Hybrid Music*

"Clarkson grabbed the reins for *My December*, aiming for angst over saccharine kisses." – *Philadelphia Weekly*

Kelly wrote "Never Again," the first single, after becoming upset with herself for acting silly over a guy who didn't deserve her. The single peaked at #8 on *Billboard's Top 100*.

"It's my most bitter song," she laughed.

"Sober" marked the CD's second and final American single. Kelly's favorite *My December* song states that everyone has one weakness that could spur an addiction.

"It's a sad song, but it's also inspirational," Kelly told *CosmoGirl*. "I've never been addicted to narcotics or alcohol. It's more about the idea that everyone has some addiction."

One unreleased track entitled "Irvine" became a quick cult favorite. Toward the end of her *Addicted* tour, the singer nursed a broken heart and felt physically and emotionally exhausted. For the first time ever, she canceled a fan meet-and -greet following an Irvine, California, show.

"I had reached my lowest point," she told *The Daily Mail.* "I thought: 'I don't want to smile or talk about myself, or do a photo shoot. I don't want to do anything.' Four or five years straight caught up on me. Even though I love my job, I couldn't do it all the time."

During her life's lowest point, the depressed singer locked herself in her dressing room's bathroom and cried uncontrollably. The shattered performer prayed for guidance and wrote "Irvine." Unable to perform the personal song in a studio, she recorded the number at home.

After Kelly emerged from her depression, she worried about having disappointed fans that night. So months later the considerate singer hosted a free concert for those ticket holders.

Kelly began the *My December* tour that fall. She performed 37 dates across the United States, including three sold-out nights at New York City's Beacon Theater. After Seattle's Paramount Theater appearance, a fan uploaded a *YouTube* clip of Microsoft cofounder Bill Gates rocking out at the concert! When Kelly finished the tour's North American leg, she hit Melbourne, Stockholm, Amsterdam, Helsinki and more. When reviewing the show, *The Buffalo News'* gushing review ultimately nailed Kelly's appeal.

"What made her performance special and unique were Clarkson's amiability and the conversational tone she used when talking to the audience. She is a friendly person who hasn't let fame go to her head. Clarkson shared personal stories and poured her heart and soul into every song she sang."

MISS INDEPENDENT
(Glenn Harris PR Photos)

Upon the American tour's conclusion, Kelly returned home to Texas to spend the holidays with family and friends. The devoted aunt enjoyed playing with her nephews and nieces. She also loved picking her sister's brain about new artists on the music scene. Alyssa had fantastic taste and discovered bands long before anyone else had heard of them.

As Kelly celebrated the new year, she reflected on the past twelve months. Despite the public struggles, 2007 felt like a success. The singer loved her job, and even when it brought frustration or heartache, she wouldn't trade it for anything.

MY DECEMBER TOUR
(Adam Bielawski PR Photos)

"I'm a real low-maintenance girl."

CHAPTER 6
"A Natural Woman"

Despite Kelly's big success, she remained an average girl next door - sort of. The superstar wasn't exactly girly when it came to fashion.

"I hate shopping for clothes," she told *The Sunday Mail*. "I'd rather go to the Apple Store and get cool gadgets."

When selecting an outfit, the high-profile artist never over thought her decisions. After all, she was a girl who once wore a Target sundress on live television!

"If I want to wear jeans and a shirt, I'll wear that," Kelly shrugged. "If I want to wear a dress, I'll put a dress on."

The singer didn't wear much makeup, except for Elemis' skin care products. After a shower, she would blow dry her hair, slap on Yves Saint Laurent lip gloss and apply mascara.

"It's frightening when you see celebrities with makeup all the time," she told *CosmoGirl*. "People see me without it all the time, so when I finally put some on, it's a shock that I can actually clean up."

One thing Kelly always had, though, were her two dogs, a black Labradoodle Joplin and white Maltese named Security.

"I love my dogs more than most human beings," she laughed. "They're awesome and they're my cuddly little friends on the road."

When Kelly went home, she lived very low-key. Admittedly, though, the adjustment to a normal life took time.

"The [bus] is normal now," she told *Cosmopolitan Magazine*. "I get home and I'll be like 'What do I do? There's no call sheet. Why isn't there catering here?' It takes a good five days to get into your routine, like going to the grocery store."

Days off began with Special K Red Berries cereal. Then she returned phone calls and emails. If her buddies didn't answer, Kelly hung up. She hated her speaking voice and didn't want it recorded! The vocalist even used an automated outgoing greeting, finding the recording process too stressful.

"It's the worst talking voice ever," she laughed.

Sometimes Kelly lounged on the couch watching reruns of *I Love Lucy* or *Ally McBeal*, or she popped in the DVD of her favorite film, *Gladiator*. When the singer watched television, she admitted to one quirky habit. The TV's volume needed to rest on an even number. Odd numbers made her skin crawl!

"It's weird," she laughed. "I don't know how I have friends."

Sometimes Kelly and her friends went somewhere for food and conversation. An ex-waitress, the singer left generous tips to the hard-working, underappreciated servers. When selecting a restaurant, Kelly especially enjoyed a good Italian meal. Mostly she cherished catching up with her buddies.

"I'd rather be with friends who have the same values as me than try to be part of some fashionable scene," she told the *Daily Mail*.

At the end of a day, Kelly snuggled in bed with a juicy novel. Sometimes she revisited her favorite book, Charlotte Brontë's *Jane Eyre*. The avid reader also liked Jane Austen novels, especially *Mansfield Park*. When she preferred a modern work, she read *The Hunger Games* series or a *Twilight* book. The performer once became sleep deprived because she couldn't put down *Breaking Dawn*!

"Every girl is obsessed," she laughed to *Contactmusic*.com. "I went to Cancun, Mexico, for New Years with friends and we were laughing because every female at the pool had one of the books from the *Twilight* series."

Meanwhile, Kelly's family spent much time at her animal rescue ranch. The caring family helped amputee goats, blind dogs, horses with colic, etc. Alyssa named one llama - Dolly Llama. Some animals were matched with adoptive families.

Kelly took on rescue responsibilities, too, visiting one animal shelter so often that she knew the workers by name. The singer typically saved animals who were days away from being euthanized. On one occasion she adopted a cat named Marilyn. The adorable feline loved sleeping on her new owner's chest, always purring happily.

Over the years many people naturally expressed interest in Kelly's love life. The singer even saw her name erroneously linked to stars like Justin Guarini and Nick Lachey. For a while she just stopped thinking about dating altogether.

"I give up," she told *The Associated Press*. "It's too hard. It sounds cliché to say 'I'm too busy,' but I really am."

Besides Kelly had so many other dreams to explore. For instance the musical theater fan hoped to star in a Broadway show someday. She even sang *Grease*'s "Hopelessly Devoted to You" at concerts and talked of one day doing *Funny Girl*.

AMERICAN SUPERSTAR
(Bob Charlotte PR Photos)

"I've always been that person who thinks anything is possible," Kelly told *CosmoGirl*. "I can fly a plane. I can do whatever I set my mind to. I'm the youngest. Everyone looks at the third one as the runt who can't do anything. That stirred rebellion in me--that feeling that I'm going to prove you wrong."

PERFORMING FOR FANS
(Janet Mayer PR Photos)

"I was never the most popular girl in school and I've never had guys falling over themselves to go out on a date with me. I'm fine with that and happy with who I am."

CHAPTER 7
"You Love Me"

Kelly had done many daunting things. She'd sung before millions while dealing with laryngitis, endured Simon Cowell's scrutiny every week and performed for the pope. Come again?

During his first United States trip, Pope Benedict XVI visited Yonkers, New York, to deliver a speech urging youngsters to avoid drugs, spurn materialistic attitudes and seek life's greater meaning. Then he watched as Kelly sang an emotional version of "Ave Maria."

"I was so excited to sing for the pope," Kelly told *People Magazine*. "It's been a dream to perform 'Ave Maria.' To have that dream come true on such a special occasion is a blessing."

Later that year Kelly and Reba McEntire united for the *2 Worlds 2 Voices* tour, a 24-date North American journey. The duo shared the same band in an intermission-free show. The modest singers always liked one another but they became very close on the tour, even hiking in Yosemite together!

The star-struck Texan adored singing with her hero. When Reba took the stage, Kelly provided background vocals. When Kelly held the microphone, Reba sang backup. Sometimes the pop star would be singing "Never Again" and peek at the country singer rocking out behind her. Was this really happening?

Every night when Reba performed her set, Kelly studied her idol carefully. She learned so much from the legend.

"There's a certain vocalist that tells stories so beautifully and she's one of them," she remarked.

Kelly even returned to acting by guest starring on Reba's self-titled sitcom as a television intern who dreams of becoming a weather girl. On the superstar's first entrance, the studio audience greeted her with hearty applause.

"I'm just very grateful that Kelly came on the show," Reba gushed. "It's been a special treat for all of us."

In March of 2009, Kelly released her fourth studio album *All I Ever Wanted*. She'd originally entitled the work *Masquerade* but other artists released similar CD titles, so she named the album after track five. The title also described the singer's career fulfillment. She cherished the amazing opportunity to record music and write songs.

The album's bright cover featured Kelly wearing a leather jacket and surrounded by vibrant colors. It represented a new look for the singer who often wore dark clothes.

"Everyone has been trying to put pink on me since I started seven years ago, so now I've given in," she told the *Daily Record*. "I was dark before but now I've embraced a new *Charlie's Angels* kind of superhero vibe. It seems to work."

The much-anticipated album hit number one on *Billboard's Top 200* chart, and critics also lauded it.

"It is a shiny, happy collection of club-worthy hits." – *The Seattle Times*

"The album is a generous helping of the Kelly so many love." - *Los Angeles Times*

RCA released "My Life Would Suck Without You" as the album's first single. The bouncy song reunited her with songwriters Dr. Luke and Max Martin —the talented men behind her massive hit "Since U Been Gone." At first the tune didn't fit her stylistically, so the threesome reworked it.

"It became a different song from how it started," she remarked. "We changed the point of view, and other things, because we had to make it more Kelly Clarkson."

"My Life Would Suck Without You" premiered at number 97 on the *Billboard Hot 100* and shot to number one the following week. Its meteoric climb set the chart record for a single's biggest jump to the top spot. The song received additional exposure when the television show *Glee* covered it.

"It's fantastic," raved *Rolling Stone*. "The early favorite for single of the year."

"I Do Not Hook Up," the album's second single, stressed the importance of taking a relationship slowly. Singer/songwriter Katy Perry originally penned the tune but handed it to her friend instead.

"Quality to quantity," Kelly told *Access Hollywood*. "That's the point of the song."

"A giddy power-pop nugget," claimed *Digital Spy*.

The third single "Already Gone" chronicles a girl gently ending a relationship. *Entertainment Weekly* called the haunting tune a "soaring, impeccably constructed power ballad."

All I Ever Wanted also included the Eurythmics-influenced "If I Can't Have You," which the *New York Post* called, "one of those tunes that will timelessly live on any pop rock playlist for centuries." In addition, fans flipped for the effervescent "I Want You," a 1960's retro tune.

ALL SHE EVER WANTED
(Robin Wong PR Photos)

"This is my happy song," Kelly joked during concerts. "So deal with it!"

The *All I Ever Wanted* tour kicked off on October 2, 2009, in Connecticut. The show played the United States, Canada, England, Germany, South Africa, Australia, Indonesia, Singapore and South Korea. Not surprisingly, the main attraction's stellar vocals and sweet personality drew big crowds and tremendous reviews.

"Clarkson's pipes place her in the upper echelon of vocalists, and perhaps explain why she doesn't resort to any of the glitz and trickery that help some artists camouflage their deficiencies." – *Boston Herald*

"Her confidence as a performer, and her skill with giving every ounce of emotion she has into her songs stands out, every bit as much as her powerhouse vocals." - *Atlantic Weekly*

"Clarkson does what her peers are too afraid or too compliant to industry bosses to do - play a concert that lets the audio rather than visual elements cause the gasps." - *The Standard*

Kelly loved touring for two reasons. She treasured playing live and found it educational to visit other areas of the world.

"I've learned something from every place I've visited," she told the *Daily Mail*. "I know it's expensive, but without travel you're in your own tiny bubble, disconnected from the world."

Obviously Kelly had an enormous collection of fans. Yet the girl who still wore Van Halen shirts also admired several artists, like Florence and the Machine and Adele.

"[Adele] probably thinks I'm insane because I talk about her too much," Kelly laughed. "I love her. She's so talented. I love anyone that can be that vulnerable with music. I read all her interviews. She's so quirky. I just think she's super cute."

~~~~~~~~~~~~

In early 2010 American country singer Jason Aldean put the finishing touches on his fourth studio album, *My Kinda Party*. He had a power ballad duet entitled "Don't You Wanna Stay" and wanted Kelly to sing it with him.

Luckily the star loved it and agreed to record it. The duo debuted the song at the *44th Country Music Association Awards* to great acclaim. The song shot to number one on country charts and became the most downloaded collaboration ever.

Jason uttered high praise for his song partner. The proud father loved that Kelly always treated his daughters sweetly. On several occasions the two sang the song on talks shows and usually celebrated afterward with a good old-fashioned meal.

Constant travel finally caught up to Kelly, though. For the second time in a year, she developed walking pneumonia. Her body demanded rest by physically shutting down.

"I love working, but at the end of the day you've got to take care of yourself," Kelly told *Closer Magazine*.

So the superstar went home and rested for six straight months. It was a vacation no one could claim was undeserved.

COUNTRY STAR
(Chris Hatcher PR Photos)

"Never mind trying to be bigger and better than everyone else. Just be the best 'you' that you can be – and have fun along the way."

CHAPTER 8
"Before Your Love"

On October 21, 2011, *Stronger* hit stores. Extremely proud of the effort, Kelly nicknamed the work "The Cardio Album" because every track contained a constant driving beat.

"I worked really hard on it," she revealed to *MTV*. "It's my best album to date."

"The album is about empowerment," Kelly continued. "It's about relationships we encounter. It's about overcoming hurdles and bad days and celebrating what we do have."

"It's a perfect representation of my life," the singer added.

A big proponent of live performances, Kelly wanted the CD to sound like an actual concert. To achieve the sound, producers eschewed auto tune and other aides.

"Mr. Know It All," a sassy tune about a woman who educates a man, became Kelly's first single. The singer loved the song from the first listen, citing its soulful, rhythmic pop nature. Fans liked it, too, giving the singer her ninth top-ten hit.

"It was unlike any song that I've ever come out with," Kelly explained on *KellyClarkson.com*. "Usually we go with an anthem, guitar-driven song. This is very different, and I was really into it. It's super sassy. The theme is very empowering."

"'Mr. Know It All' features one of the most impressive female pop vocals of 2011," raved *About.com*. "Kelly Clarkson's technical mastery of pop vocals has few current peers."

When recording the song, the singer recalled an ex-boy-friend. She referred to the mystery man as "The Stinker."

"Why did I date him?" the baffled performer wondered.

"Stronger (What Doesn't Kill You)," the album's second single, quickly shot to number one on *Billboard's Hot 100* and also became a huge hit in Asia, Europe, Denmark and elsewhere. The upbeat tune about conquering adversity featured a catchy dance hook that had listeners bopping along.

"I knew when I heard 'Stronger' for the first time that it was going to be a huge song," Kelly told *The Republic*. "The writers did a great job of capturing a memorable anthem with a powerful message."

The song's emboldening theme prompted young cancer patients at Seattle Children's Hospital to create a music video chronicling their fight against the disease. The inspirational clip went viral, earning over three million *YouTube* views. The moved singer taped a message for the brave youngsters.

"That was amazing," she raved. "It made my day. It's making everyone else's day. Everybody's talking about it. It's so beautiful and meaningful. Thank you for sharing it with us."

Meanwhile Kelly hit the road with the *Stronger* tour, playing over 50 dates worldwide. She gave each show a unique spin by taking song requests on *Twitter*. Famous covers included "Perfect," "Beautiful," "Nothing Compares 2 U," "Somebody That I Used To Know" and "Lose Yourself."

The superstar also updated followers through her *Twitter* account on nearly every leg of the tour. Kelly enjoyed direct access to fans and loved chatting with some of her over three million followers. One evening the performer invited fans to hang out with her.

"Okay, everyone that sees this in Nashville, meet us at "Larry's Lounge" asap!!" she tweeted. "Karaoke and fun times for everyone 21 and above!! Bring it!!"

The down-to-earth free spirit loved meeting the fans who accepted the last-minute invitation. The group sang all night long. Thankfully, no one oversang their song. Kelly usually cringed when some people used karaoke to prove they were a serious singer!

To pass time more easily during the tour, Kelly and her band created a book club. The bookworms gathered to discuss stimulating novels, like William R. Forstchen's *One Second After*. When people called the readers geeks, they just laughed.

The friends also played various video games. Kelly became obsessed with *Guitar Hero*, a game that allows players to simulate guitar riffs to famous rock songs.

"I'm not gonna brag but I might be amazing," she smiled.

Meanwhile "Dark Side," *Stronger*'s final release finds a girl asking a guy if he can love her despite her flaws. The artist loved the tune from the moment she first heard it.

"I'm going to need that for my album!" she exclaimed.

"Her soaring synth-pop ballad defines what love's all about: knowing your girlfriend's a little bit crazy, and still not running away," wrote *Entertainment Weekly*.

Sadly Kelly's favorite *Stronger* track "You Love Me" never saw a release. The song tells someone that she'll recover from the pain they inflicted. The vocalist channeled Tina Turner when recording the feisty number.

Kelly kicked off 2012 by singing "The Star-Spangled Banner" at the Super Bowl. After her performance she ran into her manager's son Brandon Blackstock. Also Reba McEntire's stepson, he guided Blake Shelton's career.

Kelly liked Brandon very much. The divorced man loved practical jokes and hailed from her hometown. When he asked her on a date, though, she asked for her manager's blessing.

"Go for it," Narvel encouraged. "Y'all are both great."

The couple scheduled their first date on February 11, 2012. Shortly before Brandon arrived, Kelly learned that Whitney Houston had died. Did her hero's death signal a bad omen for the evening? No. In the end, the couple chatted all night like lifelong friends and began a romance. Brandon owned a pilot's license and often flew to visit his new girlfriend when she was away on business.

A devoted father, Brandon had a son and daughter from his previous marriage. Kelly adored the children. She took his six-year-old son and eleven-year-old daughter on many fun outings. On one occasion the foursome received the VIP treatment at Disneyland!

The best part about Kelly's new boyfriend? Brandon felt more like a best friend than a boyfriend. The singer adored spending time with him more than anyone else.

"I feel very fortunate," she told *Redbook*. "I love working, but now it's more about sharing my time with someone else; I finally found someone I love to do that with."

KELLY IS STRONGER
(Janet Mayer PR Photos)

On May 24, 2012, Kelly became a mentor on *ABC*'s new singing competition *Duets*. Four superstars collaborated on songs with two unknown singers. The winner would receive a Hollywood Records recording contract. John Legend, Jennifer Nettles and Robin Thicke comprised the other star advisors.

"I find two people I believe in, sing with them every week and help them accomplish their dream," Kelly gushed.

"You can be in this business and help someone," she told *Redbook*. "I want to be that person they can trust. I'm that person who understands them, who they can talk to or cry to."

In the end Kelly guided California college student Jason Farol to a third place finish. Her effective coaching helped the shy young man gain confidence and stage presence. After the show ended, he even performed with her on tour.

Some naturally wondered if Kelly might appear as an *American Idol* judge someday, but she dismissed the possibility.

"I would never do that," she said. "I'm not good at telling people how to do something. I'm good at showing them."

However Kelly still watched *American Idol* any chance she had. Her favorite contestants over the years included Allison Iraheta and Megan Joy, whose tattoo artwork she really loved.

In fact, Kelly watched many singing competitions. Her friend Blake Shelton appeared as a judge/mentor on *NBC's The Voice* and she rarely missed the show.

"I want to audition so badly," Kelly giggled. "I want to see how many chairs turn around!"

In related news, Simon Cowell had left *American Idol* and began his own talent show called *The X Factor*. It seemed every major network now produced a singing show, but Kelly didn't believe the surplus of competitions harmed one another.

"I don't think that hurts any of the other shows," she insisted. "That's like saying other female artists would hurt my career. That's ridiculous. There's room for everyone."

Regardless of the show, the first *American Idol* champ was often asked about the secret to success on a singing competition.

DUETS AD
(ABC TV)

"It's all about song selection," she claimed. "People have amazing voices but they pick the most horrible songs that do not showcase them at all!"

When Kelly tired of reality shows, she watched scripted dramas, like *Castle*, *NCIS* and *Bones*. The singer also loved *Nashville* starring Connie Britton and Hayden Panettiere as feuding country singer rivals. It helped that the star now lived primarily in that city and loved country music!

In late November Kelly released *Greatest Hits: Chapter One*, a 17-track compilation containing hits from her ten-year career. The CD also featured three new songs, "Catch My Breath," "Don't Rush" and "People Like Us."

Kelly debuted "Don't Rush" on the *46th Annual Country Music Association Awards*. The joyful love song, featuring Vince Gill's background vocals, expresses the bliss of spending the day with a loved one. Excited to record the tune, the vocalist would never have related to it before meeting Brandon.

KELLY THE MENTOR
(ABC TV)

DUETS' MENTORS
(ABC TV)

"If I don't write the song, I have to have experienced it," she explained. "If someone would have sent me 'Don't Rush' a year ago I would have gone, 'Okay that's super cheesy. That will go in the cheese pile that I'm never going to record!'"

Listeners quickly embraced the song, along with Kelly's new hopeful attitude. "Don't Rush" enjoyed a healthy life on the *Hot Country Songs* chart.

Meanwhile "Catch My Breath," the album's lead single, became her 11th million selling song. Kelly co-wrote the smash as a reminder to herself to stop and enjoy her accomplishments. When the songwriter struggled writing the bridge, she thought of Brandon. Suddenly lyrics about making time for loved ones sprung from her pen.

After a successful album, television show and tour, Kelly then took her own advice. She went home and caught her breath.

"We get one life. Make sure that you're living it how you want to live it."

CHAPTER 9
"Thankful"

On April 24, 1982, Kelly turned 30 and happily welcomed her life's newest stage.

"The best word for your 20s is searching," she told the *Celeb Factory*. "Whether it's political views or religious beliefs or who you're dating, your 20s is life changing. I'm looking forward to the 30s being more chill, relaxed and easy going."

Kelly marked the event by going blonde, but the adage about some hair colors having more fun didn't apply to her.

"I always have fun," she shrugged. "I don't care what color I have."

About nine months later, a nation watched U.S. President Barack Obama be sworn into a second term. Kelly sat nervously a few feet away observing the historic moment. In a few minutes she would sing for the nation. Seated beside her, Brandon gently squeezed her hand.

"Your hands are freezing," he whispered.

"I'm so cold," she replied.

The vocalist fretted about her upcoming performance. Cold weather often affected vocal chords. She slipped her hands into her pockets lined with hand-warming pouches.

"I've rehearsed enough and I've practiced enough," she silently reassured herself. "If I mess up, I'm human."

After her introduction, Kelly shook the President's hand.

"I'm so nervous," the performer told him.

When Kelly reached the microphone, she smiled in disbelief before delivering a thrilling "My Country, 'Tis of Thee," which garnered a standing ovation. Afterward President Obama gave her a gentle peck on her check.

"Well, nervous looks good on you," he smiled.

Later that evening Kelly and Brandon attended a celebration at the White House! Decked in a strapless floral Oscar De La Renta gown that she'd been dying to wear for months, the singer laughed at all the tulle under her dress, which made maneuvering quite difficult!

In personal news, the girl who once uttered "I give up" about relationships had found true love. Weeks earlier Brandon had proposed with a gorgeous 6-carat canary diamond ring.

"What?" she asked. "Are you for real?"

Emotions overwhelmed Kelly. She laughed, cried and laughed again. Meanwhile Brandon looked red and nervous.

"Are you going to put the ring on my finger?" she asked.

"You actually haven't said yes," he replied anxiously.

Oops! Of course she would marry her best friend! Moments later Kelly called her mom with the good news, while Brandon phoned his parents.

"I'M ENGAGED!!!!! I wanted y'all to know!!" Kelly tweeted the next day. "Happiest night of my life last night! I am so lucky and am with the greatest man ever :)"

The no-frills girl began planning a wedding. Despite a life in the spotlight, she harbored one particularly strange fear about the big day.

"I'm terrified of everyone watching me walk down the aisle," she admitted.

Needless to say, Kelly eyed the big day with her usual sharp perspective and great sense of humor. She only became stressed when narrowing down her guest list.

"My fiancé has a thousand family members, and I have seven," the bride-to-be joked.

Whatever happened, Kelly wanted an intimate wedding. She even eschewed time-honored traditions, like bridesmaids and other attendants. Instead, Brandon's daughter would accompany her down the aisle.

In the meantime, Kelly's assistant created a *Pinterest* page for the wedding. The famous artist often joked that others seemed more enthused about the wedding than she did.

"I'm not a Bridezilla," the performer insisted to *People*. "I'm the opposite."

In fact, Kelly often questioned the tremendous work that a wedding required. All the planning seemed like an enormous amount of effort for just one day!

"I don't understand why we aren't eloping," she confided to the *Daily Herald*. "It's a lot of details and I've never been that girl."

A WOMAN IN LOVE
(ABC TV)

Luckily for Kelly's sanity, she and Brandon took a break from wedding planning to attend the *55th Grammy Awards*. The popular singer even nabbed a cool souvenir when *Stronger* won Best Pop Vocal Album. The diverse showcase beat out fierce competition from Florence and the Machine, fun., Maroon 5 and P!nk.

On March 5, 2013, *Billboard* made big headlines, when they ranked the top 100 *American Idol* singles of all time. Astonishingly, Kelly composed half of the list's top 20 and four of the top five!

The Billboard Top 100 American Idol Singles

1.	Kelly Clarkson – "Since U Been Gone"
2.	Kelly Clarkson – "Stronger (What Doesn't Kill You)"
3.	Jordin Sparks with Chris Brown – "No Air"
4.	Kelly Clarkson – "Behind These Hazel Eyes"
5.	Kelly Clarkson - "Breakaway"
6.	Phillip Phillips – "Home"
7.	Kelly Clarkson - "Because Of You"
8.	Kelly Clarkson – "My Life Would Suck Without You"
9.	Carrie Underwood – "Before He Cheats"
10.	Daughtry – "It's Not Over"
11.	Kelly Clarkson – "A Moment Like This"
12.	Jordin Sparks – "Tattoo"
13.	Daughtry – "Home"
14.	Clay Aiken – "This Is The Night"
15.	Ruben Studdard – "Sorry 2004"
16.	Kelly Clarkson – "Miss Independent"
17.	Elliott Yamin – "Wait For You"
18.	Carrie Underwood – "Inside Your Heaven"
19.	Kelly Clarkson – "Already Gone"
20.	Kelly Clarkson – "Walk Away"

Despite the major accomplishment, Kelly always insisted that she didn't achieve all her success by simply winning a singing competition. Once *American Idol's* final confetti fell and television cameras turned off, the hard work actually began. Success was an ongoing pursuit.

BELOVED SINGER
(Janet Mayer PR Photos)

"The show just gives you your 15 minutes," she remarked. "It gives you the chance to be seen on television. It's what you do afterwards that really counts. A lot of people just want to be famous. If that's your goal, it's not going to be long term. Anyone can be famous. It's called *YouTube*."

After every album sale was tallied... When the concert tours' attendance numbers were recorded, one thing remained certain. Success had never spoiled the sweet girl from Texas. Ten years after Kelly first appeared on *American Idol*, the words Paula Abdul once used to describe the humble performer still rang true.

"There's so much that comes together in becoming a superstar," Paula exclaimed. "We embrace you. We feel like we know you. You're dorky. You're adorable, and you know what?

I just love you, I just love your personality, your spirit and your voice is unbelievable."

And that's exactly why we still love Kelly Clarkson today.

ESSENTIAL LINKS

The Official Kelly Clarkson Site
www.kellyclarkson.com

Kelly's Official Facebook Page
www.facebook.com/kellyclarkson

Kelly's Official Twitter Account
twitter.com/kelly_clarkson

Kelly's Official MySpace
www.myspace.com/kellyclarkson

Kelly's Official Vevo Channel
www.vevo.com/artist/kelly-clarkson

RCA Records
www.rcarecords.com

American Idol
www.americanidol.com

DISCOGRAPHY

The Smoakstack Sessions Volume 2
Greatest Hits: Chapter One
iTunes Session
The Smoakstack Sessions
Stronger
All I Ever Wanted
My December
Breakaway
Thankful

KELLY ROCKS
(Paul Froggatt PR Photos)

ABOUT THE AUTHOR

Christine Dzidrums holds a bachelor's degree in Theater Arts from California State University, Fullerton. She previously wrote biographies on Joannie Rochette, Yuna Kim, Shawn Johnson, Nastia Liukin, Gabby Douglas (a 2012 Moonbeam Award winner), Jennie Finch, Missy Franklin, Idina Menzel, Sutton Foster and The Fierce Five, the 2012 U.S. Women's Gymnastics Team.

Her first novel, *Cutters Don't Cry*, won a 2010 Moonbeam Children's Book Award in the Young Adult Fiction category. She also wrote the tween book, *Fair Youth*, and the beginning reader books, *Timmy and the Baseball Birthday Party* and *Timmy Adopts a Girl Dog*. Christine also authored the picture books, *Future Presidents Club* and *Princess Dessabelle Makes a Friend*. She recently competed her second novel, *Kaylee: The 'What If?' Game*.

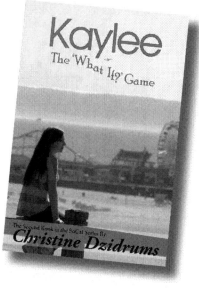

2010 Moonbeam Children's Book Award Winner! In a series of raw journal entries written to her absentee father, a teenager chronicles her penchant for self-harm, a serious struggle with depression and an inability to vocally express her feelings.

"I play the 'What If?'" game all the time. It's a cruel, wicked game."

Meet free spirit Kaylee Matthews, the most popular girl in school. But when the teenager suffers a devastating loss, her sunny personality turns dark as she struggles with debilitating panic attacks and unresolved anger. Can Kaylee repair her broken spirit, or will she forever remain a changed person?

Theater fans first fell for **Sutton Foster** in her triumphant turn as *Thoroughly Modern Millie*. Since then the triple threat has charmed Broadway audiences by playing a writer, a princess, a movie star, a nightclub singer, and a Transylvania farm girl. Now the two-time Tony winner is conquering television in the acclaimed series *Bunheads*. A children's biography, *Sutton Foster: Broadway Sweetheart, TV Bunhead* details the role model's rise from a tiny ballerina to the toast of Broadway and Hollywood.

Idina Menzel's career has been "Defying Gravity" for years! With starring roles in *Wicked* and *Rent*, the Tony-winner is one of theater's most beloved performers. The powerful vocalist has also branched out in other mediums. She has filmed a recurring role on television's smash hit *Glee* and lent her talents to the Disney films, *Enchanted* and *Frozen*. A children's biography, *Idina Menzel: Broadway Superstar* narrates the actress' rise to fame from a Long Island wedding singer to overnight success!

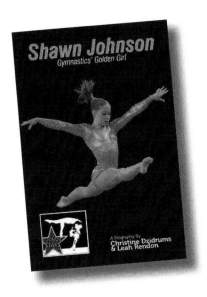

Shawn Johnson, the young woman from Des Moines, Iowa, captivated the world at the 2008 Beijing Olympics when she snagged a gold medal on the balance beam.

Shawn Johnson: Gymnastics' Golden Girl, the first volume in the **GymnStars** series, chronicles the life and career of one of sport's most beloved athletes.

Widely considered America's greatest gymnast ever, **Nastia Liukin** has inspired an entire generation with her brilliant technique, remarkable sportsmanship and unparalleled artistry.

A children's biography, *Nastia Liukin: Ballerina of Gymnastics* traces the Olympic all-around champion's ascent from gifted child prodigy to queen of her sport.

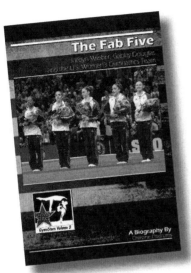

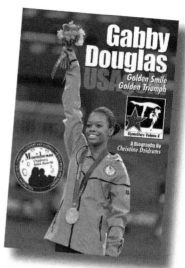

Meet the five gymnasts who will represent the United States at the 2012 London Olympics. *The Fab Five: Jordyn Wieber, Gabby Douglas and the U.S. Women's Gymnastics Team* tells each team member's life story as they rose from young gymnasts with big dreams to become international superstars of their sport. Discover the stories of **Jordyn Wieber**, **Gabby Douglas**, **McKayla Maroney**, **Aly Raisman** and **Kyla Ross** as they aim for gold in London!.

At just 14 years old, gymnast **Gabby Douglas** left behind her close-knit family in Virginia Beach, Virginia, to train under famed coach **Liang Chow**. The girl with the golden smile believed her sacrifice would someday lead her to Olympic gold.

A children's biography, *Gabby Douglas: Golden Smile, Golden Triumph* will grab readers as they experience the thrilling path the popular gymnast from the Fierce Five took on her way to becoming Olympic Champion.

Ashley Moore wants to know why there's never been a girl president.

Before long the inspired six-year-old creates a special girls-only club - the **Future Presidents Club**. Meet five enthusiastic young girls who are ready to change the world. *Future Presidents Club* is the first book in a series about girls making a difference!

Meet **Princess Dessabelle**, a spoiled, lonely princess with a quick temper. When she orders a kind classmate to be her friend, she learns the true meaning of friendship.

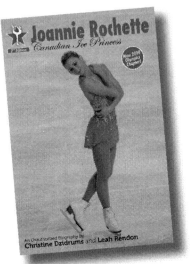

Jennie Finch fell in love with baseball as a four-year-old when her mother started taking her to Dodger games. A year later, her parents signed her up for softball lessons and the young girl was instantly smitten. As a youngster, Jennie dominated travel softball and later became a star player at La Mirada High School in Southern California. During her time at University of Arizona, she set an NCAA record with 60 consecutive wins. Blessed with remarkable pitching ability, good looks and role-model sportsmanship, Jennie became a breakout celebrity at the 2004 Athens Olympics, where she captured gold with her team. *Jennie Finch: Softball Superstar* details the California native's journey as she rose from a shy youngster playing in a t-ball league to becoming softball's most famous face, a devoted mother of three and a legend in women's sports.

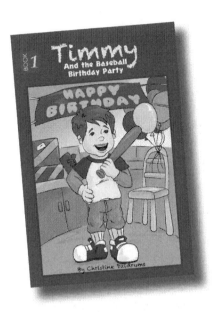 

Meet 4½ year old Timmy Martin! He's the biggest baseball fan in the world.

Imagine Timmy's excitement when he gets invited to his cousin's birthday party. Only it's not just any old birthday party... It's a baseball birthday party!

Timmy and the Baseball Birthday Party is the first book in a series of stories featuring the world's most curious little boy!

Timmy Martin has always wanted a dog. Imagine his excitement when his mom and dad agree to let him adopt a pet from the animal shelter. Will Timmy find the perfect dog? And will his new pet know how to play baseball?

Timmy Adopts A Girl Dog is the second story in the series about the world's most curious 4½ year old.

Twelve-year-old Emylee Markette has felt invisible her entire life. Then one fateful afternoon, three beautiful sisters arrive in her sleepy New England town and instantly become the most popular girls at Forest Springs Middle School. To everyone's surprise, the Fay sisters befriend Emylee and welcome her into their close-knit circle. Before long, the shy loner finds herself running with the cool crowd, joining the track team and even becoming friends with her lifelong crush.

Through it all, though, Emylee's weighed down by nagging suspicions. Why were the Fay sisters so anxious to befriend her? How do they know some of her inner thoughts? What do they truly want from her?

When Emylee eventually discovers that her new friends are secretly fairies, she finds her life turned upside down yet again and must make some life-changing decisions.

Fair Youth: Emylee of Forest Springs marks the first volume in an exciting new book series.

Made in the USA
Middletown, DE
07 April 2020

88528216R00060